SCRAPBOOK MAPPINGS OF MY COUNTRY

SCRAPBOOK MAPPINGS OF MY COUNTRY by Peter Weltner © 2021

Marrowstone Press, © 2021
All rights reserved

ISBN: 978-0-578-83143-5

With a deep sense of gratitude, I thank Patricia McCarthy, its editor, and W. S. Milne of Agenda for their generous and heartening support of my work.   PW

SCRAPBOOK MAPPINGS OF MY COUNTRY

SCRAPBOOK MAPPINGS OF MY COUNTRY by Peter Weltner © 2021

Marrowstone Press, © 2021
All rights reserved

ISBN: 978-0-578-83143-5

With a deep sense of gratitude, I thank Patricia McCarthy, its editor, and W. S. Milne of Agenda for their generous and heartening support of my work.   PW

SCRAPBOOK MAPPINGS OF MY COUNTRY

PETER WELTNER
poems

> How long at the corners of the street
> the cars delay, we wait
> for the promised, the promised,
> for the promises that carry us home.
>
> Robert Duncan,
> from *Writing Writing* (1952-1953)

MARROWSTONE PRESS

For
Atticus Carr
and
Robert Mohr

my partners through life

Table of Contents

I
South

Holderness Swamp   1
Natchez   2
Tupelo   3
Panama City   4
Sewanee   5
Ithaca   7
Savannah   8
Siloam Springs   9
Roanoke River   10
Merrimack Valley   11
Stable's Creek   13
Grafton   14
Raven's Dance Woods   15

II
New Jersey and New York

North Plainfield   19
Brookside   20
Times Square   21
Columbia Heights   22
71st Street at Madison Avenue   23
2nd Avenue and 52nd Street   24
Bayview Cemetery   25
College Hill   26
Root Hall   27
Root Glen   29
Cambridge   31
Battenkill   32
Carnegie Hall   43
Greenwich Village   35

III
Northeast and Canada

Ashburnham   39
South Boston   40
Cambridge   41
Springfield   42
Far North Coast (1)   43
Far North Coast (2)   46
Hartley's Cove   47
Matane   48

IV
Texas and the Middle West

Paris   51
Del Rio   52
Dyersville   53
Russell   54
Central City   55
Hatton   56
Northern Idaho   57
Dream Lake   58

V
Pacific Coast

West Hollywood   61
Newport   62
San Pedro   63
Santa Cruz   64
Lawton Street Beach   65
Shoreline   66
Land's End   67

The Marina   68
Headlands   69
Knoll Woods   70
Wilderness Fire   71
Sebastopol   72
Columbia River   73
Tacoma   74

VI
Pilgrimage

Wandering Rocks   77
Cana   78
Boulder Woods   79
Elsinore   80
Tibhirine   81
Clingmans Dome   82
Lake Euphemia   83
Catawba   84
Temple Gate   85
Emmaus   88
Hamilton Lake   89
A Last Wilderness   90
Home   91

I
South

Holderness Swamp

Bald cypresses in a black water swamp,
seldom seen, remote, knobbed roots
thick and gnarled, gray-brown bark
lichen-splotched, limbs thin as sticks
a boy might whittle to fish with.
At noon, it swelters, the air damp,
wet from summer. Orange-spotted newts
sun on rocks by banks overgrown
with swamp grass and reeds. Tin-
flat, a silvery white sun pierces
through clouds that float away,
thin as filaments in a spider's web,
eastward toward the Atlantic until
gusts of wind force them up higher
in the sky, dwindling like smoke trails.
The cypresses' scaly seeds are fat,
bloated, purple-brown, its leaves red-
copper. The air grows still, more
sultry as yellow flies dart about,
buzzing in the quiet we row through
stunned, unable to stay here, no history
to speak of, inhumanly beautiful and tragic.

Natchez

They should have been allowed to grow old
gracefully, they believed, to thrive, then rest
peacefully, their lives as foretold
by the natural order of things, blessed
by tradition, happily
content, wealthy, privileged,
a tribe of sorts, a family
whose standing was safely sheltered
by noble homes, their lives at one,
confluent with the river's,
always flowing, yet ever changeless. What passion
for life, what stories residing beside
its waters gave them. But they'd lied to themselves, denied
its terror, how the shackled,
beaten, dead bodies it carried
were the Mississippi, were the history
the river bore before pouring it forgotten into the sea.

Tupelo

In a collapsing, weathered house, a wasps' nest
dangles from shingles a dingy spare-
tire gray like the splintering,
peeling clapboard. Why is he there
idling, sitting
in a rented car, unable to rest?
Kudzu entangles pillars and posts.
Weeds choke the gate. Why should he care
his face is gauzy white like a ghost's?
He knows he's old. His childhood home is a ruin. His hair,
once shiny as tar, is mop-gray. Imagine a boy naked,
swimming in a lake fed by run-
off from an upstream dam. What has led
him back? The sweet smell of hay under an August sun.
The taste of well water at twilight. One moon, one night, never regretted.

Panama City

Long lines outside diners, on sidewalks,
parking lots crowded, beaches packed.
He must practice patience. No one talks
to him anymore. Life is stacked
against him, the weight of it he'll carry
all his days until he's grown too tired
and frightened by the effort, too mired
in shame to bear it. Lying's no use, no good.

Why should the wasted beach bum he
is stay in a world made for the young? Why should
he feel compelled to praise a surfer-
kid who, snake-like, sloughs off his wet
suit as if peeling old skin away? Let
him showoff his beauty. So what? Fear
is mostly the same as pride or vanity,
isn't it? And he fears what people might see.

Every night, he wakes at two or three.
Like a blissed-out monk, he sits crossed
legged on his bed, comfortably
naked despite his ragged body,
a man beset by the love he's lost
still needing to be the cool kid, the cute boy
on the beach, chanting dreamily, Come sweet baby
Jesus, come back my darling, my own Buddha joy.

Sewanee

His happiness might easily have lasted longer.
Sunlight blistering trees,
scorching leaves. Acorns falling,
Wind-torn limbs pinging,
ringing on cedar shake roofs.
Squirrels, cats, birds. Their claws
scattering bark, climbing trees. Storm-blown
twigs, sprigs scratching windows. Dark
massed clouds blanched by lightning
white as cotton. A raspy breeze
sweeping through grasses, rustling
hay fields, rattling rows
of ripening corn bent
by rain, bowing for a while
to the torrent's onslaught as it
flooded the sun-battered, hard-packed,
cracked ground the boy loves
to lie on even when, soaked deep-down,
it melts to mud, clay clods
oozing like slime off his hands,
the loam-sweet odor
clinging to his dirty fingers for days.
Life should have been like that day always,
the whole simmering summer lasting always,
the sky at night nearly unbearable,
too huge, too beautiful.
Stars flaring red. Meteorites
crashing, burned up. The humid,
swampy, viscous air throbbing,
pulsing to the beat in his ears,
of his racing heart as he waits

for no one, wants for nothing,
eager, insistent that it never
stop, not ever, the overbearing,
suffocating, relentless heat of it,
the fever, the swelter, the sweat
pouring out of him, the ache, the need,
the passion inside him more fiery,
wilder, fiercer than even the earth
gripped in the bliss of July that one day was

Ithaca

A boy steps out of sunlight into the shadows
of an entryway, stares at a stoop hidden
in the half-dark, glances toward meadows,
the road that bypasses his father's garden,
flowers abundant as hothouse's. The morning
is balmy, apple trees sweetly blossoming
late in the spring. Why does he feel the sting
of guilt for dreaming nightly of leaving
everything, everyone he knows? His youth
is restless, given to wandering, his true home
who knows where? The breeze billows sheets hanging
on the line like sails unfurling. He yearns to roam,
to seek adventures, discovering new places, meeting
new people for the tales he'd tell later, freed
from the need for his stories to stay faithful to truth.

Yes. It is a late, spring-fragrant, Southern morning.
The sky is peaceful, clouds calmly
drifting westward toward rolling hills. Nothing
is harder than to abandon your country
and your family to journey to unknown
places. The corn's grown tall as he is in the pasture.
Hidden by the stone
wall behind the barn, he feels safe, unseen, sure
of his destiny. Lets Paul's fingers touch his lips
brush his hair, smooth the blond fuzz
on his cheeks and chin as he grips
his shoulders tighter, his breath warm on his skin. No alarms
this time. No warning signals. Just why he must go that was
shown him. The voyaging. The wanderings. The trips,
the journeys he'd imagined himself taking when held in Paul's brave arms.

Savannah

Cicadas' raspings, hotter than the air.
The moon's light, entangled in live oak trees.
Red-eyed in headlights, a possum flees
across the highway. Fireflies flicker.
up, down, crosswise. Bat cry. Owl
cry. The night's a tunnel, an underground
cave, no way out. Hounds howl
in a yard. Moths buzz loud
as a saw. Streetlights gleam an oily
yellow long past midnight.
Steam rises like smoke off a damped fire
still smoldering. The sea's sickly
smell is strong as a salt lick's. The sticky sweet perfume
of magnolia, gardenia thickens the air. It is not right.
It has all arrived too soon,
the city besieged by a summer heat
come to defeat
it unless a storm in late afternoon
fights through to relieve it of its ungallant occupier.

Siloam Springs

Her obit says she's gone home to the Lord.
Six children, ten grandkids survive
her. For fifty years she adored
her husband, vital, alive
one day, dead the next. In heaven,
they'll be singing by the throne
of the Lord, kith and kin
beside them, shown
their way to glory if that's truly how her story
has ended. Who did she live for
really? I know better. Not the man
she called her husband. Her sinning began
the night she met Bill Purdue whose son she bore
and claimed was Ed's. And never thereafter could either be happy.

Magnolia, lilac in the air, an orchid in her hair,
fine crinolines, a linen wrap, pearl earrings,
boys' whispering sweet nothings
to her as she curtsied, a girl without a care
in the world, free to dare
to do what she wanted to, who ran rings
around her suitors until she'd grown too old
to play act her assigned part. She told
me her real story once. I find
it surprising still, all the lies she left behind
her. Life often swings
between extremes. Dying on her bed, "No heaven for me,"
she says while smiling, seeming not to care.
"Death's only more lies," she says. "More denials. More secrecy."

Roanoke River

The rain quits at dawn just as the birds begin
their singing. A young man wanders to the river,
sits on a boulder, feeling kin
to no one, nothing, the scrabbling water
from a storm overflowing the banks as he grasps
a branch of a sycamore that toppled early in
the deluge, clasps
it tighter as its trunk slides deeper
into the flood. Two crows caw
at squirrels shinnying up a pine. Sunlight, harsh and raw,
seeps through clouds. His hound brays at a sliver
of the moon as he tosses a clay clod in to test the power
of its flow, how far the Roanoke might carry him through low
brush banked by forests past farmlands to where he wants to go.

Merrimack Valley

As a starless night darkens, the wisp of a moon
dips behind a wall of spindly trees into
a silence audible as music. Might it untune
the sky, too, as Dryden's ode says will come true

some day in the future. Time will stop, apocalypse
irrupt. How joyously Handel's music celebrates
its arrival, timpani beating, trumpets blaring the eclipse
of all things. The end of time. The world it translates.

The dead shall live, the living die. But what
can it mean to untune? What do dissonance,
disharmony sound forth? Or what unthought
thing does silence make heard to human consciousness?

The genius of a river is its steady flow. But suppose
people have succeeded in opposing its
freedom, subdued it, subjected it to laws,
their rules, trees downed, woods clear cut, mining pits

dug, sacred grounds paved over by highways,
industrial plants built along every bank
dumping into it wastes that greed lays
on its bed like seed or silt, poisonous and rank.

On a moonless night of what sparse wilderness
still abides in the Merrimack Valley,
amidst birch, boxelder, sugar maple, sassafras,
hemlock, ash, imagine one tree frail and elderly,

withered as most ancient trees are now, like a delphic
priest, one of nature's wisest, prophesying a city's
fate is that of the wilderness, its foliage's thick
canopy understood too late, only vague shadows, the sky's

last light denied it, untuned by moonset, utter darkness. Hear,
in the black silence of that forest, the ode
the tree sings in spite of fear, the woods' trusted seer,
oracle of sleep and the river. How long as forever they have flowed.

Stable's Creek

Near an almost forgotten battleground, farmers reap
wheat. A highway runs close to the fields.
Mustard and darnel flourish where sheep
graze, the earth rich and loamy, what it yields
worth the work it takes. A frail, stooped woman
is picking wildflowers. She looks sad,
like someone who has lived alone too long. What began
her day has ended in madness. Her lad,
who died a century after
the battle, fell here, she's sure. Her face's
darkened by his shadow. She hears him cry, "Mother,"
as he stands beside her, gazes
into her eyes. No war is ever over. He pleads, "Forget me."
But she can't forget. Her boy died here. Look by the creek. Near that tree.

Grafton

Some people do return to the town, though afterward
wonder why, the downcast look
of friends who still live here, haggard,
dressed in ill-fitting clothes, not a book
in sight, each intent on something
mysterious, hard to see, faraway.
I recall a pretty girl staring at a thin gold ring
she wore on her ring finger, alarm or dismay
distorting her face. Ours is a town without imagination,
some say. She appeared to be afraid
of something. Or someone. I might have asked her what
or who, but feared I'd be intruding. My son
was born in Grafton long ago and there was laid
to rest. I can see her face, but not my boy's. When I think of that,
when I picture our home as it was, I wonder if he'd ever really played
in the park no one dares go close to anymore, the one the town's locked shut.

Ravens' Dance Woods

It is rumored that on winter
nights ravens dance
secluded in woods, prance,
cavort where
no moon is able to look, their clacking
voices mocking
the grace they lack,
startling trees, streams,
forest creatures
as if they are under attack,
as if in dreams
or in the outer reaches
of the heart their dancing teaches
those who see it the strangest artistry is nature's.

II

New Jersey and New York

North Plainfield

He revels in everyday mornings, the common-
place, birds early feeding, cars on the street,
kids walking to school, the warmth of the sun
through his bedroom windows greet-
ing him each day. The contentment
he feels, the peace he finds in ordinariness. So what
if his life means nothing to others, lunch spent
in the cafeteria, office tasks, paperwork that
no one else will do. So what if paradise
turns out to be as dull or monotonous
as life can sometimes feel. His imagination defies
repetition and routine. It is us,
he thinks. Our secret. Yours and mine. What no one
knows but us. My dream man. My soul mate. My passion.

Brookside

The sun is raw, cold and white,
fields glazed with frost
all morning long, a sting, a bite
to the air, the last, wind-tossed
leaves scattered in loose piles.
A man steps over stiles,
listening to the call
of geese flying south, free
to leave winter
behind them. It is the century
that's gone bad, banal,
not nature in its profundity,
nor the wilderness he'll enter
more deeply soon, content at the end and happy.

Times Square

1.

Illuminated marquees, neon signs,
streetlights, cop cars flashing,
a fat moon trapped between building
and billboard, crowds, long lines
of guys outside a bar, its door
red velvet drapes a few peek
through to see if it's real or a poor
mimic of what its sign vows, the reek
of booze and smoke, thicker than
haze or fog, bored male strippers spotlit
by a filtered flood that colors bodies
a fiery blue brighter than the sky's
at dawn when the city wakes him like a man
easily satisfied by the lust that lights his spirit.

2.

Strolling alone, his black jacket
too big for him, his slick hair
drenched, right hand in a pocket,
left scratching a ruddy cheek where
it itches, his shadow like a ghost
stalking him in a slight rain
or heavy drizzle, he looking lost,
like someone struggling to sustain
his dreams, the sidewalk glassy as
he steps aside to let a bum pass
him, a clean wintry shine in the air,
a boldness to it, no cars, taxis to dare
or dodge that might fight him for the Square
he cockily struts through, new boy in town, proud of his ass.

Columbia Heights

From his apartment, he can see the bridge,
its cable curved like a hull, its lights beacons
to the North Atlantic, promising passage
to faraway, happier places. Illness weakens
him, his body hurting as it continues to fail.
Shining through a window, the moon paints,
in shadows, two masts and a furled sail
on his floor. Or shackles, iron constraints
that lock a body in place. The light from stars
plays and dances on the silvery flow of the river
as a tugboat moors, waves lapping at the dock. Pain mars
everything. He knows that well. But he would save
any man who might try to drown in its strong, icy water.
He would assure him life is good. Uncertain of it himself, not brave.

71st Street at Madison Avenue

The art of it, how all thought belongs together
as part of one era, unchanging, her maroon
upholstery, rose-rust velvet curtains, umber
wood work, the ripe musty smell, the gloom
of rooms whose doors look more inviting closed.
She keeps the lamps lit low delighting in how
the glow appears to cling to things unimpeded,
though never imposed, her library's row after row
of books' bindings shining as if a candle's flame
illuminated each title lovingly gold-imprinted. Her cat,
porcelain black, arches his back on a bookcase,
leaps across a rug and claws at a flaw in its pattern.
Dressed in summery white, sighing, she stares at
him while he shreds its loosened threads. It will soon be her turn
to leave all she cares for in glorious tatters. For which disgrace
she does not apologize or cast on her lessers any of the blame.

Second Avenue and 52nd Street

Sometimes the early morning light on city streets and sidewalks is so fine
it allows the past to be ignored for a while, intensifying the present
by heightening colors, the green of awnings, the blue of strewn ribbons
gliding over heads, the yellows on window signs, the sparkle of sugar buns
enticingly on display in a pastry shop, by clarifying the shape of words,
the black and white of signs, the forms of awnings or shades, the birds
flying easily, soaring above the streets' hubbub and bustle, cries and cheers,
by lovingly elucidating each human face, intensifying precisely the line
light draws at dawn between night and day when the city starts to sound
exultant—honking cars and taxies, ringing cellphones, pounding, deafening
jackhammers, foremen barking orders, workers yelling curses back—while
each moment passes by faster than people do racing past each other, yester-
day's fears or failures less pressing now they have something awaiting them,
somewhere to go, what is happening this instant more insistent than what's
been left behind, tears after an argument, a child's bedtime grumblings, the
joys of a compliment, a night given to pleasure, the soothing dreams of sleep,
the neighbors below making love shouting louder than drunks in a dive
bar. Why should yesterday matter? The city's morning glare, the shadows it
casts off its high rises and billboards: so much to know of what it means to
be is to hear and see what every daybreak gives unasked for to everyone as if
through God's grace, freely by its untold mercies.

Bayview Cemetery

Grandparents, parents, two brothers, an aunt buried
in our ancestral tomb overlooking the Hudson.
From the heights, I can watch people being ferried
over the river, though not as it once was done—
with coins for the ferryman to carry them
securely across to wherever it was the dead
were meant to voyage to. Mowed grass, trim
hedges surround chipped gravestones by the lead-
gray monument to my family's hopes and pride.
Soft moss, lilies, red poppies border a boxwood wall.
Charon, look at me straight. I keep a silver dollar
securely in my pocket or by my bed. Someday, I'll hide
it on my tongue for you to take as payment. Oar me as far
as wherever it is you go across the Styx. But wait for my call.

College Hill

Friday

The photo is old, with an eerie golden glow
to it, two streaks of bright red and ultramarine,
like stripes of flags or waving pennants, flow-
ing from each upper corner onto a scene
in the midst of a winter storm. The light is hazy,
as if filtered by gauze or the thin veil released
when the earth beneath the snow exhales slowly
into a cold that turns its warm breath fleece-
white, the flakes minuscule as droplets of mist
not falling but shimmering, suspended in air like fog.
Like the piles of snowbanks, the Gothic buildings persist
in their fervid Romanticism, their aura of epilogue
in a photo shot to convey what it means to store memories
as a solitary young man gazes on the shifting drifts and stark black trees.

Saturday

The next day, the snow has covered the world in a white
lovingly shadowed by bare trees and old dolomite
buildings, a bright, yellowed light like a favorite moon
I slept under often, pale as a face seen through a window.
The sky is clear as summers at sea, a few clouds, soon
to sail off, lingering over the valley. There is no sorrow
here, nothing to regret, a quiet, peaceful morning
I might listen to like music being played far away,
barely heard. It is like living in parentheses, tomorrow
repeating the rites of yesterday, a clarity like returning
as I do looking at a photo taken after the storm not to stay,
but to find what I want to discover under the snow
if something might be rescued from banks so high, hiding below
it and the ice: a book of poems, a tie, a wool scarf, a love letter, any memento.

Root Hall
   (To the Memory of Professor Edwin Barrett)

Reciting Shakespeare, he assumes all the rôles,
voices, this one Hotspur's: "Swear me, Kate,
like a lady as thou art, a good, mouth-filled
oath...." And we—hungry, expectant souls
as we are—watch as he puts down his book, wait
for the next gesture, his arms spread wide, thrilled
by the theatricality of it as he winks, hit-
ting just the right note, smiles, proclaims, "Ladies
don't say 'I need to go to the little girl's room.'
Real ladies speak plainly, say, 'I need to take a shit.'"
And we laugh wildly, in an uproar, a laugh that frees
us as poetry means to do. To liberate, to presume
it knows us better than we know ourselves. Ed
picks up his weighty blue bound Shakespeare. Becomes Falstaff. Ned.

Or Macbeth. Romeo. All the rest. His most admired part
we agree, is rapt, entrancing Cleopatra. One guy
said he got a hard-on listening. Despite his flamboyance,
Barrett teaches us to see, to read each scene, the art
of it more profoundly. His laughter, his jokes are a sly
way of disguising a sadness in the man. An avoidance
(perhaps) of tragedies inside him he lets his theatricality
reveal and hide at once. Hamlet brooding, Lear on the heath.
I recall on the day of Kennedy's assassination how we
watched him crying, weeping loudly as he quit Root Hall,
to walk home down the hill, in the early winter chill each breath
he took like ours visible in the cold, in the voiceless hush of all
we were thinking and could not say as we watched the news on TV
like a tragic Shakespearean play, a great one fallen, a ruined royal family.

Many of us are gone now, too, of course. It is fifty six years after
that day, or nearly so. A year before, Kit and Cam had died
in a crash during a snowstorm on the New York thruway.
Young, we learned how serious death is. Not even Ed's laughter
could laugh it away, not that he would try to. He often sighed
after reading a comic passage, for, however witty, every play,
every work of art is beset by great sorrow, hilarity in its way
just another form of grieving. I recall as well the last night I slept
on campus or tried to sleep excited by our graduation the next
day. I woke up in my room to stare out the window. A noise kept
sounding in my ears, like distant music, sweetly distorted, that beck-
ons or calls you out, like the moon that May night pretending the light it shed
was snow falling in late November, startling me half-awake out of bed
to see Ed spreading Puck's flowers upon us so none of us could leave, none ever
wept.

Root Glen

Collegiate Gothic dorms, classrooms, fraternities
built from local dolomite. Others of brick, smoke-
blackened by punitive winters. A few white New England
clapboard houses with wooden Doric columns, wrapped porches.

A Victorian mock mini-castle with a spired mimic
turret, romantic as a Scott novel. A cottage,
its oldest building, preserved as a relic for
secret meetings by select societies. Wide swards

of grass carefully tended for soccer and lacrosse,
a golf course, quads' rolled lawns, a football field
with its bleachers seating no more than two hundred,
a stadium in miniature on a campus so carefully composed

it could be read like a lyric poem articulated by
glens, meadows, and haunted woods. A hill's steep
descent to village taverns, the climb back up sobering.
A three story chapel, lead paned windows, clocks

and chimes in its steeple marking lives and classes,
the passage of time as the college chose to
display it, an orderly place safe for becoming
well-read, thoughtful gentlemen, the essential

texts needed for inherited tasks. Homer, the Bible,
Shakespeare, Milton, Wordsworth, Conrad. Greek, Latin,
German, French, Spanish. Philosophy. The core
sciences. Math. The history of the world offered

in four years to us living outside it. Choral singing, theater.
(Shakespeare, Jonson, Beaumont and Fletcher,
Beckett, Christopher Fry.) Houses parties, days and nights
consumed by beer or scotch or stingers. Autumn as written

or inspired by Keats, sensuous, melancholy, enflamed
by the heat of its colors. Winter snows piling up to
second stories, drifts white as seas stilled by moonlight.
Spring arriving tardily, too late, delayed like a love letter

lost in the mail until suddenly it appears, opening itself
in your hands, it seems, its words more joyous than you
might have written yourself, more surprising. And you delight
in it, in every spring, despite how briefly each stays faithful.

For tragedy, our teachers if challenged might intimate, belongs to chaos,
the dark beyond learning's borders they have spared us from,
like Renaissance humanists saving the past from its violence,
as Mattingly taught us, by restoring its ancient books and languages.

How could I not believe as I did, as knowledge used to, that life
becomes comprehensible, even beautiful if you read enough
and write about it with humility? We were assured change was
an illusion if seen through the timeless. If we'd been deceived, so be it.

Years after, I still owe a debt to what some now call lies. I am trying to re-
member, my long lost friend, how true life looked the March night we held
gloveless hands while crossing a bridge in Root Glen, the creek iced over as
together we quoted Coleridge, the hornèd moon with one bright star within
the nether tip.

Cambridge

Spring arrives later every year. Winter
thaws slowest where tall trees cast
shadows on the banks of the river
as it bends and narrows a mile past
the bridge. A wizened, ruddy man
leans on a rail, noisily sucking plums
while a truck hauls logs across the span.
He spits a pit into the water, hums
merrily. The road up the mountain
is too arduous, slippery and sheer,
for him to risk anymore. Plum juices
stain his jacket. The world is dear
to him, clear, plain-spoken, wondrous.
He hates to think of leaving it, the loss
of all he has seen or known, though here
where he's home the river floods as it chooses.

Battenkill

It's famous. "Best trout fishing stream in America."
Here, the river doglegs, forming a pool Eakins'
boys would have loved if they'd lived near, flat,
man-sized rocks to sun on, a hemp rope, high
as a silo, tied for years to an old oak branch
still able to support two or three grown men
swinging over the waters, frothy where deepest,
to dive or cannon-ball in. Summer is such
a kingdom on the Battenkill. Idling bird song.
Folks on inner tubes floating by. Beyond Gerald's
and Bob's, it curves past bridge and silent mill.
In the corner of yards, on the border of farms,
headstones stand erect or lie half-buried,
well-kept or moss-covered, some chiseled with dates

older than the Battle of Saratoga. Small American
flags, some wind-shredded, memorialize the fallen.
Its planks peeling like infested redwood, fathomless
pits gaping between boards, a barn forms
a backdrop of sorts to a terrace, one of three
edged by brush and rocks, that descend to the water.
Fenced on both sides by fragments of stele or bits
of monuments no longer standing or long torn
down, its path narrows like an isosceles triangle
to a point where a girl's beautiful head carved,
etched from granite rests on a tall wood plinth.
The woman who posed for it now is dead, lying
only a few miles away under her own stone,
guarded fancifully by giant sculpted dogs.

Memory is a heraclitean flow none can cross
the same, unchanged, each time. I barely met
her, spent much of our one afternoon together
talking Faulkner with her and her husband, saying
how in his art landscape, place, is always part
of us and the past races past us faster than
the future can try to catch up–or something
like that. Who knows anymore? The face she wore
was an old woman's graced by joy like Hals'
Malle Babbe, an owl, wise to age, also darkly
perching on her shoulder, the girl she was
and is in the sculpted portrait still visible, as if
life were endless, streaming like the Battenkill
under winter's ice, fighting to stay river.

Carnegie Hall

Walking from Carnegie Hall into a fierce blizzard,
I miss my bus's last stop, try near Fifty Fifth
to catch another, walk down slick stairs toward
the subway, board it though its crowded with
Christmas shoppers, discover its going south
not north too late, escape, outside the entrance
take a right, each breath like ice in my mouth,
my face freezing, pass a bar with dance
music playing, a truck's tires whining as they grind
in the slush, streetlights buzzing, a bitter wind
wailing past a row of tenements, through high wires,
radio static seeping out a bizarrely open transom,
the singer's voice distorted to the noise of crackling fires
as I listen, succumbing to the snow, to being nowhere home.

Greenwich Village

1.

A warm May morning. A jogger waves as he runs
past, flags flapping from a brownstone, bright
with rainbow colors. A taxi, flashy pink and white,
dashes through traffic, zigzagging lanes. The sun's
being squeezed between two high rises. Waiting
for the light to change to cross into the park,
I hear, near dock's edge, a tug's horn baying
like a sick dog. In a corner playground, darkened
by shadows from a looming brick building,
children rock on teeter-tooters, young men shoot
baskets, a grown woman twists chains on her swing,
giddy with laughter as she twirls. Tonight, The Magic Flute
plays at the Met, an opera so humane in its happy
sad music it glows, radiant as this city in spring, noble and ordinary.

2.

I walk from a dance recital at the City Center into a blizzard,
misread where the bus stops on Forty Third Street,
and descend into the subway instead, though it's hard
to know which train I should take. The snow's turned to sleet
when I emerge from under ground into the Village,
Washington Square packed with people frolicking
in the storm, having fun despite the cold, whatever age
they are. Christmas grows near. A cop car is whining
far away. A slightly sloshed drag queen skids
on ice. Dimmed streetlights blink and sputter, wind
sighs down through a corridor of brownstones. Kids
salute each other on their way home. Sweet music seeps
through open shutters, Schubert I think. One weeps
for joy sometimes without reason. How good this world can be. How kind.

III

Northeast and Canada

Ashburnham

Yellow birch, red alder, red oak,
white pine, moosewood,
marsh fern, lady slippers,
bluebeard lilies, poke-
berries, toadflax: spring's things, now winter's
own to claim, as nature says it should.

Chunks of ice drift down the river. Each day
is colder, darker. The snow's
icy crust crackles. The mossy grass is frozen. Gray
clouds blur the sun. A sharp wind blows
through a thicket of brush and pine
where a rack
of stag's antlers and splinters from a snake's spine
poke through the snow cover, bone brittle and muddy black.

South Boston

Roaming the halls of a Catholic nursing
home, a defrocked priest, cheeks red,
arms wrapped round his chest, sing-
song singing words instead
of saying them, opens his eyes
wide and shouts, Have mercy. Buttons
and strings hold his pajamas up. He tries
to hide the spots on his robe. The sun's
low, not at all how it shined on Easter.
He shuffles through a wheelchair lined corridor.
He is thirsty, searches for a working water
fountain. His soul is grief-stricken. Poor
Father, a nun murmurs. He stares at her. Poor everyone.
Everyone undone.

Cambridge

It was raining yesterday in Cambridge. It is
raining today in Cambridge, rain and more
rain. He pulls up a window shade, fixes
his collar, stares down at the quad, the door
he'd locked after he'd left, the boy with curly
blond hair and lavender eyes who strolls
on the sidewalk umbrellaless, then boldly
struts, wearing no raincoat or jacket as he rolls
a joint, oblivious of the cold and wet,
grinning, waving back at him just as his pudgy
roommate, a morning drunk, after struggling to get
his key to work, stumbles in. What more is there to see
or to say? Things equal to the same thing are equal to each other.
Tomorrow, it will rain again in Cambridge. There's philosophy in weather.

Springfield

The sun sets slowly below the canopy
beaming, its light webbed by trees,
branches, limbs, their leaves
fiery,
incandescent before
shadows retake the woods. A brown
thrasher, two warblers soar
into the sky, blown
higher by winds. A meadow of yellow
and lavender flowers, leather leaf, purple berries,
salal, thistles glistens like moonlit snow.
When he hears his mother call him back, the boy hurries
to hide. It is not her love he fears. Nor her kindness he runs from.
But the night he flees into, unheeding her pleas, her cries to hasten home.

Far North Coast (1)

1.

A man who's not unhappy, but desperate
in his heart, strolls idly by the Atlantic,
looks up to watch birds he can't
identify migrating, flying higher,
crane-like in their easeful soaring,
feathers the pale gray-white
of beach pebbles dawn-lit in shallow pools.
He wonders why, as the flock fades
into clouds drifting west, the choppy sea
shines most gloriously in the earliest morning,
though veiled by shrouds of mist and swirling fog.

2.

There is an unnamed season in the midst
of early winter, one day pleasantly
warm, the next gripped in an Arctic
cold, skies obscured by dense fog,
the wide eastern horizon invisible
to the eye, though he tries
to find the line that divides
one world from another anyway,
the uncertainty of where it might be drawn
somehow troubling, the ocean calmer
after storms like a man's grief gradually quieting.

3.

What high tide hides, low sometimes
reminds him of, the coast last night
swept clean of bottles, trashed cans,

paper plates, cups, detritus people
had tossed aside, this morning littered
with what the sea has thrown back,
though surprisingly washed, cleaned,
scrubbed, polished of all that had rendered
each ruined, worthless, like the child's
blue beach pail and shovel he's just discovered,
reviving the happy boyhood he suddenly holds in his hands.

          4.

His regrets are unredeemable, come and go.
He waits disheartened, sick of the trees,
birds in a plague-fraught world, wind,
fog, the long rainy nights,
though somehow he still loves life,
the gray gull resting on a pile of
charred fir logs clacking its beak,
the unleashed grizzled mutt barking at him,
the thick mist slipping over rocks
and boulders into woods unlit by dawn as morning
brightens sparse sedge and grasses neither too soon nor too late.

          5.

He is trying to think of the truly considerate
mind, what his mourning might mean
to it in a world gone awry,
half-mad, destitute, he a man
who would gladly bed down
in the earth if only it would embrace him
more gently, comfort him
as fog consoles him despite
all it hides, concealing him too, if he wants,
as if he despairs, not wanting to be found, when what
he needs is to belong to life's own, to be held again, to be cherished.

6.

There is a shelf somewhere beneath the Atlantic
no one can find. It has crumbled
away though it still influences
tides enough to make them dangerous. Loss, sorrow
are like that, each an uncharted reef ships
wreck on or that drowns
unwary swimmers because
its currents shift so fast and perilously,
like the fog, the heavy mist he walks
in most mornings now, each stumbling step he takes ghostly, unsure,
the fog dispirited as his love is, though faithful to the ways he misses them all.

Far North Coast (2)

Two white tailed kites fly past in tight alignment with the brightening
horizon, wings rippling like ribbons to crests in the air.
Crackling under foot, frost encrusted grasses cling
in patches to the narrow path. An icy sun burns through bare
clouds. The sky's a glacier blue. I feel a cold exaltation
as we shiver in the salt-scented breezes. Morning light shimmers
on the dew wet trail and trees as wild flowers open
to a sun looming over redwoods, firs,
madrones, bay laurels, live oaks whose bold, stark
outlines darken the shadows they cast toward the west,
the deep maroon crevices in the cliff walls. And so we stroll,
or loll, or sleep, never violating the silence, no wise remark
to make about life amidst such magnanimity. When it is time to rest,
let the world we leave speak like this of winter, how beautifully it chills the soul.

Hartley's Cove

Sailors. Fighters. Fishermen. Laborers.
Naked torsos. A last supper
depicting the agony
of workers, hurt bodies, sad faces
painted by thick, blunt fingers.
Boulders, mountains, pine, fir,
spruce stands, rocks, sunsets, the sea.
Earth's wound. Damaged, hurt places.
Trees, stones, birds, clouded skies.
The broken bodies those who love
them mourn for. Forks, knives,
spoons, cups, plates. A glove,
cap, jacket on racks, no longer worn.
Pray to each. Relic. Crown of thorns. Icon.

Matane

A boy's toes dig up pebbles on
the rocky beach, the wind
St. Lawrence cold, all his attention
given to what he might find.
A toy shovel, a pretty shell, a lost
coin. He wipes sleep from his eyes.
Yawns. It is early dawn. Frost
sparkles on trees and shrubs. He spies
a fisherman in his boat gliding by,
counting his catch, pike and wall eye.
The boy kicks a stone back into
the river. A black-capped tern flies
over head, a shrill, blue-colored, rue-
ful music in its cries, silenced by sunrise.

IV
Texas and the Middle West

Paris

The night he told me he was returning to Paris,
in Texas, the moon through the window
cast his shadow on our bed. I stood,
looking out, not trying to stop him. It was callous
of me, I suppose, to let him go so easily. But I know
he didn't want me to protest. We'd enjoyed a good
life for a while. But suffering inspired him, found
its best ally in him. Twice before, he'd repudiated
his hometown. His time with me was over. Now, he's
more devoted to deserts, emptiness, the hot sound
of dry wind blowing across flat lands attempting to seize
his soul, to spirit it off. A pillar of cloud, a pillar of fire leading
him nowhere, leaving him parched, denied Canaan, famished,
the promised land closed to a man who's found he's happy with nothing.

Del Rio

Its water is gritty, drying up. Awake or asleep,
nowhere. Just a wall half-built, strong
and metaphysical, steel trusses to keep
it in place, aliens where they belong.
Shallow, rusty, the river sparkles
as if gold flakes floated down it. The heat, when
winds blow off the desert, incites fevers, lulls
minds into fantasies, lets cruel delusions ferment.
Not far from town in mountains, men
slip through passes by night. Estrangement
is their way of life, hiding by day in arroyos, in a mystical,
shadowy, wasteland half light, what all
its citizens see as a scene from a gangster flick meant
to take place in landscape exactly like theirs, bleak and primeval.

Think of the film as the story of refugees, as a tragedy
told in an ordinary, unheroic way on a movie screen,
shot to be
an evening's entertainment,
a stark country inhabited by those caught between
the living and the soon-to-be dead who must consent
to be ghosts, who refuse
nonetheless to abandon the shade
cast by live oaks and bald cypresses that thrive
in the sandy, parched earth along the border,
their histories, their lives
left unreported on the news,
unremembered by history. There's no refuge from being afraid
if, from the start of it, your life has cast you in the part of a prisoner.

Dyersville

I sit on the grass, my back against an oak,
spying on them through a window. Cigar
smoke fills the room. I watch it soak
through grimy lace curtains. The two are
arguing. Has he told him? The younger
one runs his hands through his hair.
The older talks and talks. It isn't over.
The room resembles a nineteenth century
set obscured by a scrim, the staging
dated, old used clothes, the props not right.
The brother holds his head and rocks and rocks
in an antique chair. My lover is busily jiggling
his broken pocket watch. His family's grandfather clock's
bronze pendulum ticks and swings, burnished to gold by sunlight.

Russell

Locusts rasp, whirr. A fan's
bent blades flap against a tin-
thin steel guard. A dog laps
water from a bowl. Trees' long
shadows twist into snake's shapes,

The air is electric. We both swelter,
sweat beading on our skin.
The sky darkens A few gaps
in clouds force a warm breeze
to drift into our room. A cat scrapes

on a porch screen. At the first bolt,
moths beat their wings darting,
trying to fly in. Mosquitos buzz
through. A white picket fence, trellises
entangled in ivy, roof shingles flare

bone-white, galvanized, jolt
after jolt, late afternoon's blue
sky darkening blacker than tree
bark. Flattened petals look like
faces pressed against a window pane.

At last, the torrent comes, curtains
flapping against sills, the thunder-
storm fast seizing the evening
that by nighttime lets the cooling
breeze we sleep in sweep over the plains.

Central City

His face is bulldog blunt, tough,
hungry, like a boy's mug pressed against
a shop window, rough,
pugnacious, a kid fenced
in by life unlike his father who in the photo
is shown in profile, etched, incised
onto paper like a fine Victorian intaglio.
Behind the wheat field where they stand,
a three story farm house
claims the good, rich land
around it. The boy's grand-
son holds the photograph in his hands. The past is perilous,
secrets revealed in every picture.
Why families fail, what time conceals, and you, child, never to be sure.

Hatton

Call it Norway. The old country where you'd return
to join your people. Stark peaks. Fjords. Craggy mountain
ranges. Not here, in the Dakotas, where you learn
early how life mocks you, exposes each stain
you fear inside you to scorn,
despised, a troll.
So your sole trustworthy
friend is the winter, snow your faithful
partner. Last night, you dreamed
of a desert, sand, sky,
timbrels, flutes, dancing, imbibing wine that streamed
beneath a steamy sun. Yet north
is who you are. It is what you're made of. What you are worth.
Blowing off the prairie, a freezing wind calls you back. Never ask it why.

Northern Idaho

Two mountains soar in the domed shape
of pine cones seen
as on a Chinese screen, a craggy landscape,
a narrow valley winding between
cliffs and ridges. Two men pole
a skiff down a slow river
as deer stare out at them. In a clay bowl,
a woman cooks fish over a fire. A duck, every feather
sunlit and silvery, floats downstream.
High up, in a clearing, there's a wooden hut
where monks, like those painted on a scroll, dream
of Idaho, their eyes shut
to everything but paradise. What does it mean to see
mountains through their watchful eyes? What do they picture so clearly?

Dream Lake

Stone-gray hills, shallow
creeks, lupine, poppies,
cornflowers in a meadow.
Red, saffron yellow roses
lining a trail to a lake.
Three men, hard at rowing,
a storm about to break,
thunder roaring, lightning
cracking. A tall, deep-
rooted oak struck
by a bolt toppling falling
at the feet of a boy asleep
unable to budge, run, duck,
or flee from lake or tree, dreaming.

V

Pacific Coast

West Hollywood

In a fenced off backyard, by the patio, masked faces
glow scarlet from coals burning in the barbecue pit. The petals
of the fuchsias clinging to the lattices
blush pink or a brighter red. Air-fouling traces
of starter fluid mingle with the smoke. Someone calls
my name. I turn round. See a bedroom's curtains
being closed. I've been elected to guess the rôle
each guest is playing from his costume, the toll
I'm made to pay for arriving late. I take great pains
to get each right, but make mistakes. Dancing follows. Swing
your hips, throw your arms freely toward the sky.
Or dance the tango. Join a kick line. There's more jazzing
in the bushes. Who will survive the rest of the year? Who die?
I'm asked to survey the room, find the saddest eyes no disguise
or Halloween mask can hide. We're all actors in the same play where lies
are our lives. We've learned to tell them well. Yet never again will we apologize.

Newport

My favorite childhood memory is the Pacific one summer
as a sailboat briefly skimmed the horizon. The sky
was foggy, a mottled gray like a newspaper
left out in the rain. I don't know why
I thought it so beautiful. I was wearing a t-shirt and cut-
off jeans. I don't know why that matters either. Parents
should be kinder to their children. I'm in a rut
there's no way out of. My life has had its painful moments.
though none worse than now. I don't believe in god. Do you see
how the scrub brush bends westward after
storms like this one at sunset, dislodging rocks, dropping them easily
into the sea? It is hard for me to understand our days. Character
is everything, I'm told. But what does it mean, at the end, not to be?
A life that's a lie is obscene. It comes between us all. I'd like to have been a sailor.

San Pedro

At twilight, San Pedro smolders below
a sooty sky, the bridge over
the bay nickel gray, though
still shiny. Trucks, cars like ticker-
tape dots race across it. Stucco
houses glower as the sun sets.
Surfers sit on their boards, wet
suits steaming. Joggers sweat
in the heat, the Pacific calm, blue
as a pool a child might safely
swim in, few waves for surfers to ride.
Soon, a full moon will tug at the sea,
high tide pounding cliffs. It's almost suicide
to try to catch a wave then, but some still dare to.

Monstrous crests break and shatter
like glass on rocks, jarring the continental
shelf, shearing off chunks to scatter
on the beach like bits of broken coral
or ground-up shells, pieces of cliff face
mixed by the sea-surge with muscular
swells that dump seaweed at the base
of the bluffs. Next day, along the far
reaches of the coast, dawn comes, rosy-
orange and pink-hued gold, to radiate
throughout the bay an amber-tinted glow,
the brilliance of the morning like a reverie,
like a dream poised between chance and fate
of the man I loved forty years ago for a day in San Pedro.

Santa Cruz

Blinking his eyes, he flings open a window
that looks toward the Pacific. It's sunset.
Warm, balmy breezes waft in, salty
and pungent. The manzanita throws a shadow
tall as a redwood's on the beach. The air smells of sweat
and brine. A lone woman steps out of the sea.
He draws the curtains further back to let
in more of the failing light. A soft wind caresses
his face. Faint traces of birdsong fade into
the distance, like a lark's attune to the beauty
of the moment. How lovely,
how quiet the light is. How rapturous. It blesses
everything. Just to see
it, to glimpse it is enough. All that's made glorious by its brevity.

Lawton Street Beach

Close to shore, waves crash into each other,
shattering as they cascade onto the beach. A plover
picks at a bed of kelp a stray dog sniffs at warily.
Staring at the bird, a man is distracted by
the raucous pounding of the sea,
while the plover attends to nothing
but its hunger. The waves break and clash again
as gulls caw, caw, caw in warning.
Last night's storms have scattered debris
along the sandbar. The winter fog is thick
as summer's. Sleeping under a blackened blanket
a woman sticks her head out to listen to the pipers, the click-
click sound of their beaks. What has she to gain
from waking?   She is a wave breaking on shore. She is a bird trapped in a net.

Shoreline

The dawn star and a quarter moon hover, alone,
over the horizon. A harsh fall wind whips in.
The sand ripples like waves as the sun
breaks through trees in the hills. So our day will begin,
we hope, rising gently, almost
shyly from bed. Gusts have piled new dunes
on the highway. On the northernmost coast,
where the earth curves, it is still dark. Raccoons
chatter, squabble in the brush. A pencil thin line,
like a zigzag crack,
shows where the earth broke apart. There's a brine-
like taste in the air. If we could make time go back,
recant what we've done, would we be happier?
Relive the day we bravely swore neither would deceive the other?

Land's End

In a weather-darkened barn on a hillside blanketed by
thigh-high, sun-tanned golden California grasses,
on a lake reflecting the pastoral blue of a cloudless sky
untroubled by the loss of years, of what passes
now for desire, for joy, see?, there's the lost green
world of youth that once offered itself like a boy on the Russian
River rowing a canoe, swimming in the water unseen,
hidden by trees until, where otters frolicked near the ocean,
he stepped naked onto the beach right below
the cliffs and met me with a smile. How easy sex was then.
How simple. Bars. Back rooms. Guys cruising San Gregorio.
The trails and thickets of Land's End. I suppose heaven
could be like that if angels were gay, eros necessary as food
or air. Why do I seek that lost rapture now? That paradise we pursued?

The Marina

A moon-infused summer mist chills the city,
a spectral glow to it as in photos
taken during London's nightly
wartime air raids as smoke rose
from bombed out buildings blocks away
and ghosts like those
writers met wandered through the rubble
in the gap between times. It is hard to say
why a few lines of poetry can provoke the imagination
to rhyme one's life with others. Here, by the bay,
little happens that is remarkable,
yet the view from shore offers a consolation
I write about to make him stay, not to mourn
him as Jay steps out of the haze at the blare of a foghorn.

Headlands

In the west, far beyond the continent's edges,
as the earth darkens it is slowly leaving
behind long shadows of regret, its ledges
no longer able to cling
to cliff face. What word
do a people need to hear
they have not heard
before as they cower before the night, full of fear?

Let us praise the birds, we guilt-ridden people.
A thrush feeds in a garden. A glorious
Scott's oriole bathes in a puddle. A martin's plumage
shines a dazzling sapphire while it preens. Simple
and sudden, a robin or a wren rises in easy flight. What rage
belongs to birds that we might learn from? They stay here to pardon us.

Knoll Woods

Pine kindling, stripped oak logs stored in
birch bins. A rocking chair. Maple
bed, tables. Plastic windows for the cabin.
A wood panel for front door. It's a chapel,
almost, spared an altar. Plates kept
stacked in an unopened cabinet. Knives,
flashlight, watch in a drawer. Floors unswept.
Soot black walls. Crude boots. Archives
of a life. All redolent of the acrid scent
of a hearth's smoky air. Knoll Woods his shrine.
Within it, the cabin he built is modest as a tent.
His was an anonymous life, little sign
remaining of it save that which is sensed in what
a man leaves behind for no good reason. The silent,
daily things. A bar of soap. A belt. A mop. A blackened pot.

Wilderness Fire

Forest fires flare on the horizon, some flames
reaching higher than the hill or mountain
they are decimating. What are the names
given the newest ones? What pain
is alleviated by labeling each, like a sign
torn free, denying the chaos? The sun shone
at noon a smoldering red across the skyline,
like the smoky afterglow of a drone
attack on a village left desolate, a mass
of smoldering rubble no amount of water
could extinguish. In the forest, the grass
is sere, leaves curled and brittle, river
beds cracked dry. Night fevers. No one sleeps,
like a child whose mother's died, who lies awake and weeps.

Sebastopol

Birds fly far away
sometimes, further than maps know.
It is another smoky day.
She gazes out a window
at soot and ash, a pallid
sun nearly invisible,
charred trees stark, denuded.
She senses lost lives in the air's fatal
cast, dark gray and smoky. It is the disease
of fire she fears. It is dangerous to breathe
here, stifling, suffocating. These
are her days. One leaf,
lightning stuck, and a world is set
on fire. Burning skies scorch her eyes to scarlet.

Columbia River

An osprey circles for fish over a river
sparkling, silvery with trout. Rain's on its way.
A man sits in a Sunday crowded diner
as he waits, contemplating a gray
noon through clouded plate glass windows
while voices struggle to be heard over
the loud chatter of families, cooks, busily
harried waitresses. The man's lonely. He knows
no one. His life's never been content or easy.
On the sidewalk, shattered wooden cabinets,
a car's bumper, smashed cans, battered boxes,
underwear lie in a pile strewn carelessly, without regrets.
He looks out toward the big storm forming over the sea.
He thrills at the prospect. All the detritus blown away. All he was, all he is.

Tacoma

Wet, storm-splattered windows everywhere
gazing out at another dun day, a sorrowful day
somber, sober as a wake. No May meadows
greening, blossoming to play in, no calm lake
to swim in. No bracing October nights to doze
through. No last leaves to rake. No flurries
or winter blizzards. No transformative mercies. No seasons.

Only rain. More gray rain daily. The plain gray of clouds
and sea and shore, flooded gutters, sewers, rivers
soaking cities, towns drowned in rain. The gray
sound of its falling on cement or soggy ground,
the gray of boredom, the gray of pain, of never-ending
inclement hours. When will the weather change? When will
the sun be restored to its splendor? Its light rain in torrents once more?

VI

Pilgrimage

Wandering Rocks

An impoverished, blue-denim sky, gritty sun, cracked clay
for pavement in the dark outskirts of the city,
its waters poisoned. Do not stay.
Go away. You can see
how the stench of it rises
each day, the river
polluted. Who devises
the rules that lead to disaster?
In our neighborhood,
nothing lasts long. Young men leave
or grow no older. What is the good
of a life without a future? To grieve
endlessly?
To be happy
on a fine spring day: that's
my righteous politics, each an angel
at Jesus' tomb rolling the stone away. No rats,
no lice, no poisons left to kill us after together we've harrowed hell.

Cana

Ripe figs, honey, roast lamb, dates, chilled melons,
jugs of wine. 'Cana' it proclaims on the town's sign
in southwest Virginia. It's a Sunday. No one's
in sight as we pass through, no place open to dine
or drink in yet while its people rejoice in the real,
heavenly marriage awaiting them, a feast memorable
for its miracles, new wines finer than old. Is a zeal
for life possible only when holiness is translatable?
Throughout the Piedmont, lingering leaves smolder
red and yellow and orange. Soon, they'll quickly fade
to tan or brown and drop on the ground. Glories
abound in all festivities, though most are forgotten. My father
died yesterday. Tomorrow he'll be celebrated, laid
to rest. And I'll tell the few friends I have left in Carolina
whatever it is I recall best of him, the old fond hoary stories
they already know while I, distracted in the midst of his obsequies,
in my sorrow, ponder why, together, you and I confessed to a sudden, inner
hunger we'd known reading its name, driving through the Sunday quiet of Cana.

Boulder Woods

After the rain has stopped, the soaked leaves,
shaken by winds, drip, trickle steadily
onto a forest floor choked
with weeds and brush, fall's foliage already
heavy on the ground. In late October, twilight
flickers with a golden gleam deep in woods, fern trees'
fronds shining, dolomite
boulders sparkling, a bright,
glittering creek, moss on stumps and logs–
all luminous until the earth gives way to dark. I have looked
far into a woodland's shadows while tree frogs croaked
and owls hooted in a grove. I have listened late at night
to the dripping of the leaves. I have lain, sleepless, on a grassy
knoll and heard what nothing sounds like when there's nothing left to see.

Elsinore
(For Samuel Crowl on His Eightieth Birthday)

The cheering and applause quickly fade away
as Hamlet enters a darkened stage
to begin his performance. Who wouldn't say
he is the most selfless actor of his age?

So many grand reviews. So many spotlights
on him as, eyes closed, he stares
deep into his soul's confusions. Who rights
a wrong by killing himself? He truly cares

for his father, ghost or not, nor would he mourn
in a black velvet costume, a loyal son
exposing his grief, if not utterly undone
by the old man's death, revenge his lonely passion.

His words, gestures, sighs have been plotted
with meticulous care as he waits, stone-
faced, to start his soliloquy. He once said
to his public that all he wants to be known

for is as a modest man of the theater, famous
for performing himself over and over,
lost in his best rôle, an anonymous
player enacting the most tragic Hamlet ever.

Tibhirine

How a man ends his life, must it matter? It is snowing.
The monks are dressed warmly, wool sweaters,
thick coats, scarves, knit caps. The winds sting
their frost-encrusted eyes. Colder weather's
lurking as they walk deeper into the woods, their way
unsure, their steps halting, their tracks swiftly
hidden by fast falling flakes. This is their last day
on earth. They know it but somehow see its beauty
anyway, the whiteout they struggle through almost pure
light, blinding yet evoking, as silence might, a deeper
visibility. All that is is light. Behind, ever more sure
of how fine it is to be alive, they leave beds, warm water,
matins, chants, music from Tchaikovsky's Swan Lake played
on scratchy LPs. Listening to it was like joy. It was like a lover's serenade.

Clingmans Dome

Hike again through thickets of underbrush,
foxtail fern, lupine, wood anemone
to a ravine's piles of lumber and scree,
eons-old boulders. Rest there. Don't rush.
Cool off under the shade of hickory,
yellow birch, fir needles blurred by
high country mist. Cross the brook
nimbly, its thick slabs slick with algae.
Soon you'll be near the end. Pause. Look
up. You're close to the summit, journey
over. You detect faint echoes of your feet
when, young, you climbed this same steep
ridge. Try to spot him through the thicket as he whistles
back for you to reach him. Make your peace. Wave your farewells.

Lake Euphemia

Come next year, we'll not meet there
again, each to greet the other,
embracing in the meadow, bare-
boned though we now are, my brother.
The lake reflects the stride of egrets
as they wade, unmolested, in shallows
where an anchored boat's lights rest
like tired hands upon the water
or, splayed wide, a shed flight feather.
We hunt for what's left of a ruined nest,
its sticks and tiny cracked shells. Cows
low near a weathered fence. Egrets' silhouettes
shade the lake, its calm unbroken by undertows
at twilight. A life of suns is setting. The darkening air.

Catawba

A green mountain, low clouds hid-
ing its stooped granite peaks.
Still wet from a late rain
the fir trees' needles, the forest
canopy shone with a red glow
lit by the last of a setting sun.

On my bed, you lay beside
me. Twilight speaks
strangely sometimes. Of pain
maybe. Fireflies, as if obsessed,
flickered outside. It's time to go,
you said, our good day done.

Darkness calls us to darkness. I
should have slept and dreamed
of you instead of watching
the last light out my window
dying after you'd slipped away,
lured by the moon dipping over Catawba.

I never knew, as we lay together, why,
content, happy it seemed,
you let that slip of a moon, seducing
your eye, make you follow
it like some brilliant array of stars
into the dead of night woods of Catawba.

Temple Gate

1.

For those like you who must make
it across, the ways of the world
grow more difficult, all temples
strictly closed. The sky glows at dawn
as an old wavy-headed fellow
slowly walks barefoot down the hill
toward the beach, dressed in rags
blotched with mud. The slope is
long and steep. I step away as he
passes by me. His white hair glitters
in the early light. If I did not put this
down on paper who would guess
his need to find his way back home
through wisteria vines and iron gates?

2.

I write these words—swift as a breeze
blows through my windows—to keep
what is fading from fleeting further.
Outside, hawks hungrily circle antennae
on neighbors' roofs. Error is the old
man's monkish gray beard I failed
to mention, the anguish visible on
his face as he bears on his shoulder
the torn, stained comforter in which
he sleeps, the bed he lays out
on a slab of concrete as he huddles
in a doorway until sunrise comes
to hustle him away or noon rages
at his age with its numb, blinding heat.

3.

So vast is the gap between heaven
and earth that no one can say all is
well with us. I close the shutters,
dawn hurting my eyes, gauze curtain
dusty as mist, no promise of cooler
days. I no longer know who I am,
open a window facing the sea
to watch waves break, white capped
as far as the horizon. Do you recall
the basilica we visited once on
our way to L.A.? How we strolled in
its cemetery's garden as an ancient
monk with white curly hair pruned
roses, unfazed, smiling sunward unmindful of danger?

4.

Bright day, then another brighter,
brighter than sun,
brighter than noon,
brighter than vision,
the moon now set, too,
and you and I, lovers,
hiking slowly down
a cliff, a steep slope,
a ravine almost, night
after night as a white
bearded monk keeps us
company, coming, going,
leaving us to wait by a river,
leaving no trace, no map to guide us.

5.

Which way did it face? The dream,
I mean, of an ancient temple gate,
vines dangling from all four
walls, the wind through the ruins
like distant voices chanting, no
proof of anything, of course, hard
to tell where the singing came from
or if anything out there was singing
at all. When a love collapses in
the beat of a heart, it breaks
like an altar relic or sacred tablets
inscribed with fragments of names.
When a faithful soul vanishes, dusk-lit,
it shocks the earth with its absence

6.

Suppose mercy is a white cloud rising over
dry hills, a bird that sings without
yearning for the woods it flew
through, an icy stream we stepped in
hip high, the mysteries of intention.
Suppose it is my confusion of love for
you and the world, that it be no illusion.
You care for your dying aunt thirty seven
hours by plane from your home while
the air everywhere is miasmic, fraught
with danger. Suppose, why not?, the old man,
the ragged man with his comforter slung
over his shoulder, is a down on his luck itinerant
monk, prophetic of days when temples re-open.

Emmaus

Swirling winds tear and scatter petals from a garden
behind a wayside inn, a storm
over low lying hills anxious to unburden
itself of its rain, to form
itself into thin white clouds again, peacefully drifting
through skies, no more maddened
by the lightning that gashes the land, the heaving
thunder it is fated to carry inside it, saddened
to have to frighten you: like a man showing his wounds, offering
for you to touch them, still oozing, not fully healed,
wanting to let you feel how his pain
is not who he is, hoping if he revealed
them to you you'd know it is not sorrow
alone suffering brings, nor is it spring yet either, come tomorrow.

Hamilton Lake

A bright, vivid May. Thistles growing out of red clay,
ivy-entwined thickets, dogwood, backwoods in shade
and shadows, noon sun untamed, cardinals, a jay,
a scrappy feral cat squabbling with crows, a jade-

like pale green to new leaves and dew-wet grass,
chipmunks, squirrels, oaks' twisting, thick roots,
quick creeks leading to a widening lake, No Trespass
signs posted by half-sunken, rotting rowboats, newts,

tadpoles, minnows. And he, happy, swimming nude,
alone, lying after on a muddy bank, a strong spring
storm on the way, raindrops large as pebbles, his solitude
oblivious of sorrow, the beautiful promise that comes to nothing.

A Last Wilderness

A wilderness where he hid when he could from time,
from family and friends, retreating from bad news,
escaping disasters. Believe me. I'm
not saying death didn't obsess him. I possess clues

he left from his past to know better, the near total dark
of the forest where he would struggle with vines,
fight against ivy and brush, oak and hickory bark
black as duff, fungus growing from stumps to find signs

of the mammoth trees that once rose there in wet air
always drizzling, the heavy, thick canopy diffusing its bare
light, dimming it to a dusk-like shimmering bronze, the inviting
woods where he fled from death's eyes into the merciful arms of spring.

Home

Return home, boy. You needn't stay with me. Go deeper,
become more lost, if you must this late, than you
have ever walked before. Follow the birds. Hike further
in. Dare to seek from woods whatever they say is true.

Explore, though it is evening. Find a forest to go back to, to embrace,
to subdue your fears. Believe in the passion you
thought old age had denied you too soon, that trace
of the trail or path or way ahead, young, you failed to pursue

or wander far beyond for fear of the dangers. Enticing woods.
Intimations of sycamore, poplar, birch, spruce, maple, hickory,
sweet gum, pine, of wind and sun and welcoming sky. Childhood's
oak groves your soul still believes in. That ardent time. Those darkling trees.

Peter Weltner taught English Renaissance poetry and prose and modern and contemporary British, Irish, and American fiction and poetry at San Francisco State for thirty seven years. He has published twenty books or chapbooks of fiction or poetry, most recently *Antiquary, Poems and Stories*, *Vespers on Point Reyes*, *Selected Poems* 1989-2019, *Late Thoughts*, *In the Half Light*, and *Bird and Tree*. He lives with his husband in San Francisco by the Pacific.

www.ingramcontent.com/pod-product-compliance
Lightning Source LLC
Chambersburg PA
CBHW021957290426
44108CB00012B/1104